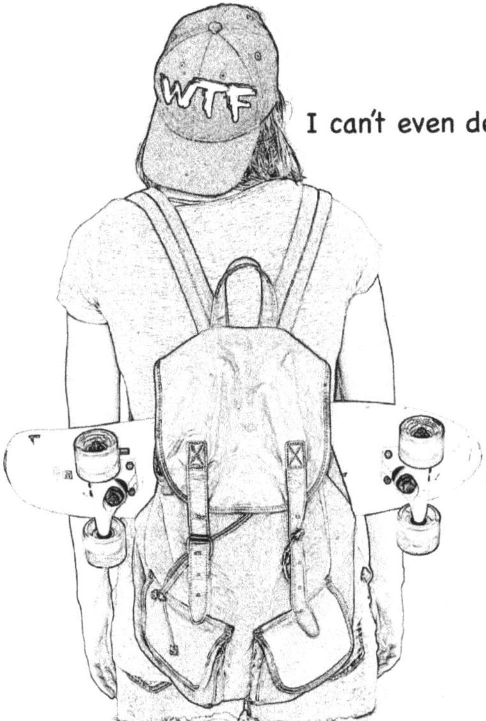

I can't even deal

Ellice De Giovanni

WTF – I Can't Even Deal
First published in Australia by Ellice De Giovanni 2018
www.sweatseeker.com.au

Copyright © Ellice De Giovanni 2018
All Rights Reserved

ISBN: 9780648308706 (pbk)
ISBN: 9780648308713 (ebk)
Details available from The National Library of Australia

Artwork by Ellice De Giovanni © 2018
Edited by Mehitabel Douglas-Drysdale

Typesetting and design by Publicious Book Publishing
Published in collaboration with Publicious Book Publishing
www.publicious.com.au

No part of this book may be reproduced in any form, by photocopying or by any electronic or mechanical means, including information storage or retrieval systems, without permission in writing from both the copyright owner and the publisher of this book.

For my Son. May you enjoy this incredible ride life has to offer you with a smile and an open heart.

Contents

ABOUT THE AUTHOR i

WTF - I CAN'T EVEN DEAL iii

PISS OFF DISORDER 1

PERIODS 14

THE PILL 28

GUYS 32

BRAIN STRAIN 38

SOCIAL MEDIA 54

RELATIONSHIPS 66

FOOD 72

LET'S FIX THIS SHIT 85

IF YOU CHANGE NOTHING,
nothing changes! 101

THE CHECK LIST 103

ABOUT THE AUTHOR

My name is Ellice. Who am I? Mmm, good question. I was a teenager, I was an athlete, I was an advanced care paramedic (and there are plenty more). I am now a fitness professional, health motivator, and author. And I am sure I will be a lot more in the future.

What I really love to do is help people; I love to share my experiences and knowledge with people to hopefully change lives. I want to help you. As a paramedic for over 10 years I have seen and felt and shut out a lot. I have also lived a life full of experiences that have led me to this point, writing this book for you. Life is a collection of experiences that expand us, grow us, teach us and mould us into who we choose to be and everything happens for a reason– YES? IT DOES!

I have personally been through and experienced all the topics I cover in this book. I came out the other side with a deeper understanding and more knowledge of how to do better next time around. So, it is my pleasure to share what I have learnt with you, in hopes it will do the same for you. And hey, pass it on. If it helps you, then share the knowledge you have learnt with others, so it can help them too: that is how we better our lives and our world.

Enjoy x x
Ellice De Giovanni

WTF – I CAN'T EVEN DEAL

This is your first step, your starting point! It is your checklist and emotional manual that will help you to answer all of those questions and feelings tumbling around in your head making your heart sad.

If this book is in your hands then it is 100% the right book for you, right now.

"Every breath hurts. Every sigh is a why. Every hour spent alone makes me feel unknown.
I have no friends. I have no love. All I have is this empty feeling.
I'm crying out for help and it's just not there. I feel so alone and no one cares.
My thoughts are so bruised and my body aches. I become numb, my breath shallow. It pierces though my heart like a broken arrow.
I need a friend. I need a hand—just a touch to show it's there.

Why can't you all see this is not really me, standing and talking. I am as distant as can be.

It's my riddled mind; it hurts all the time. Can you help, before there is no more, before there is nothing left of me to see?" 28.2.2002

I remember constantly writing poems and words down on paper when I was a teenager and young adult. I would sit alone in my room with the music matched to my mood and become lost in my feelings as they became words on paper. It was a way of dealing with my emotions, I guess. As I started to read this tear-stained, faded piece of paper written by my 20-year-old self, that I recently found, 15 years later, I was not only heartbroken for her but I also could not remember feeling that much pain or having those desperate words even come out of my mouth. I am 35 now. I grew up; I moved on and I am ok. I am not those words any more. I wish my 35-year-old self could have whispered in her ear and said, "trust me, you are going to be fine. In fact, you will be happy, healthy and so loved by friends and family. This is not all there is. You have *life* to unfold and discover. Yes, there will be hard lessons to learn along the way, but they will make you stronger and more resilient. And they will lay the foundations for a wonderful life, just like the next 35 years will do. Don't give up!"

What I can offer you, reading this, is an "I understand." I get it, and I too have been in your shoes. In those desperate, sad or angry, deafening moments, it can be hard to think straight. It feels like you are in quick sand, alone and sinking fast on a cold, dark night. But I am here to help you and show you that there is light at the end of the tunnel; you just need to know where to start. Let me be your 35-year-old self, whispering through this book to offer you some guidance and help to stop you feeling shit, sad and sorry, right now.

WHY AM I FEELING LIKE THIS? AND, IS IT NORMAL?

When you make a cake, you have to put all the ingredients in to make it work perfectly. Miss an ingredient or a step in the process, and the cake won't bake. It is then a matter of going back and seeing what you missed, so that next time you make it, your cake is the best it can be in every way. There is no difference with your body. A symptom is just the warning light coming on telling you, "hey, something is off balance, not working or needs attention, changing or fixing." Ignore the engine light and it will break down on you.

My goal for writing this emotional manual is to get you proactive about YOU. I want to help you own your health and happiness. To help you understand that everyone has the same and equal access to their awesomeness. Some people just understand their doses and ingredients better than others, and how to fix things when they don't feel right. With the help from this book, now you can too.

It is time to take control of how you are feeling and time to try to change and fix *you*, before you are palmed off and misdiagnosed like so many teens are. This will take persistence and a "want", on your behalf, to really change some things in your life and to learn and grow alongside *you*. You are the only one who has to live with you and your thoughts 24/7, 365 days a year… FOREVER! So, why not learn the secret to dealing with *you* from an early age so you can always be kicking goals in life?

This book will introduce you to important and helpful topics that can explain all the factors that could be causing you to feel shit, sad and sorry, and the solutions to help you turn the shit into better, the sad into happy and the sorry into "not anymore." And it can all be done without any invasive or expensive procedures or medications. So, let's start with these questions: are you feeling depressed? And how can you start to feel better?

The following chapters deluge into some topics, that could be the reason as to why you are feeling so shit, so sad and sorry about life right now. So get a pen handy and jot down any 'yes' moments, any insights or realisations that may come to you during these pages because you are about to experience a lot of ah-ha moments.

PISS OFF DISORDER

Pyroluria. The mirror image of depression.

Our brain and bodies need certain nutrients in order to function correctly, just like a car needs the right fuel. Put the wrong fuel in your car, or stop putting fuel in your car altogether, and it is either going to malfunction or stop working completely.

So, what are the best fuels for your body to function happily, as a normal, stable human being? Well, there are a magnitude of them, but let's concentrate here on the ones that keep your brain happy.

VITAMIN B6: The "build" vitamin

Vitamin B6 helps the body convert food (carbohydrates like pasta, bread and starchy vegetables) into fuel called glucose, which gives you energy to get up in the morning and move about. Your brain cannot think straight without glucose, and I am not talking about jelly beans or crappy sugar. I am talking the good, healthy, wholesome glucose-containing foods like fruit and veg.

Vitamin B6 also helps the body build neuro-transmitting pathways, like roads or highways within your brain and body, to enable messages to travel from one cell to another, communicating what your brain and body needs and wants.

What else does B6 do? Do you want to get the edge on school or work? B vitamins will help you do that. They help you learn, think normally and focus properly by helping the body make hormones such as serotonin, which helps maintain your moods; norepinephrine, which works to help control anxiety and maintain healthy stress levels—something you need when exams are on; and melatonin, which helps regulate your body clock, making you awake or sleepy at the right times.

Not enough B6 and you will be experiencing crazy mood swings, irritability, anxiety and depression-type symptoms (confusion, fatigue, low energy, aches and pains).

Vitamin B6 is super important for nerve function. Your nervous system consists of your brain, spinal cord, sensory organs and all the nerves that connect these organs with the rest of the body and are responsible for the control and communication of your body. Pretty important stuff!

ZINC

Zinc is the magic element that can help cure your acne, strengthen your bones, build your immunity, enhance your digestion, strengthen your heart and make you think better. It maintains your hormones, helping to balance those crazy hormonal mood swings all teens experience. Not enough zinc and you might start to lose your hair, have runny poo, poor immunity, chronic fatigue, poor concentration, poor memory or hormonal problems.

OMEGA FATTY ACIDS

Omega- fatty acids play a crucial role in the normal growth, development and functioning of your brain. They help stimulate skin and hair growth, maintain bone health, regulate your metabolism and maintain your reproductive system. Without enough omega fatty acids in your system, you can feel hyperactive and anxious, and you can experience poor memory and poor learning skills.

What sucks about being a teenager is your body is still working itself out in regards to its emotions, nutrients, moods and overall health. Unless you are a super healthy, clean-eating, Zen, stress-free teenager, there are going to be some out-of-whack issues going on inside of you—and this is totally normal. One of these issues could be pyroluria, or as I like to call it, "PISS OFF DISORDER." Pyroluria is when you have a lack of the above vitamins and minerals that we just spoke about.

So, what exactly is "piss off disorder"? Well, some might say it is just you being an unhappy and moody teenager, and others might say you're totally depressed. Well I say PISS OFF. This is serious, easily fixed and something that will make you feel so much better day to day if it is addressed right from the start.

Think of the blood in your body as the car and the passengers inside the car are nutrients, such as B6, zinc, glucose, oxygen and your hormones. Your blood's job, or the car's job, is to get those passengers to the party (your cells), and in this case, your brain cells. The car must drop them off and then pick up the excess rubbish from the cells and dispose of the rubbish via different measures, like urine, poo, sweat and carbon dioxide.

One of the waste products you need to get rid of is called HPL, or pyrrole, and this sucker likes to party to hard; it doesn't like to leave. It overpowers and dumps its toxic waste over everything, to the point where you are unable to get rid of it. Too much HPL means the party has got out of control, and all that is left is a rubbish dump, clogging up space. This means you can't pick up any more passengers, or nutrients, to drop off where they are needed, because the car is bogged in the HPL garbage that has taken over.

Your B vitamins, zinc and omega fatty acids can't join in on the fun. They become unavailable to you, and trust me, it ain't going to be a fun party without these nutrients attending.

Your brain, or the host of the party, needs glucose for energy, B vitamins to stay happy, positive and fun, and needs serotonin and norepinephrine to keep you feeling chilled and less stressed. If old mate pyrrole has taken over and locked the doors, or stopped the neurotransmitting pathways communicating, your brain is now basically starving.

Too much Pyrrole will also start to rust your car, or cells, depleting all antioxidants needed to keep you young and healthy. If the rust becomes too bad, it will stop the car from working altogether, and your body and brain will start to feel as though they are breaking down.

What is the biggest cause? STRESS. The more stressed you are, the more "piss off" HPL levels increase in your body, stealing those nutrients that need to get to the party, or your brain, to make you feel better. Poor diet. not eating enough good nutrients, alcohol, smoking and drugs, both recreational and prescribed, all contribute, placing more stress on your body, internally, therefore feeding the HPL "piss off" party pooper.

It is a vicious cycle. You may feel depressed, but it might just be that you are low in serotonin, whose job is to level out your moods. So, when you don't have that host at your party, you feel more sad, sorry and stressed which increases more "piss off disorder," which makes you feel more DEPRESSED, and the cycle goes on and on till you're rocking in a corner saying "WTF I can't even deal

Symptoms of "piss off disorder," PYRROLE, include:

Severe inner tension
Inability to think clearly
Temper tantrums
Lack of regular menstrual cycles
Acne
Low tolerance to stress
Explosive anger
Anxiety/anxious

PISS OFF DISORDER

Delusions
Migraines
Seizures
Frequent colds, fevers and chills
Hallucinations
Hyperactivity

Skin rashes
Substance abuse
Insomnia
Iron deficient (anaemia)
Abnormal body fat distribution
Loss of appetite
Allergies
Overwhelmed in stressful situations
Depression
Nervous exhaustion

Panic attacks
Nervousness
Emotionally unstable
Fatigue
Dramatic
Paranoia
Social withdrawal
Mood swings
Argumentative - likes to argue
Dyslexia
Poor memory
Eczema
Poor morning appetite
Reading difficulties
Hypersensitivity to noise
Constipation
More energy in the evening than mornings
Delayed puberty

I bet you can tick a few of those symptoms off. The question, then, is why have you never heard of this before, and why was your only available option a diagnosis called depression and then a cure: antidepressants? And this diagnosis most likely happened before checking your body's natural nutrient levels?

Unfortunately, "piss off disorder" (pyroluria) falls outside the normal mainstream medicine, due to the fact that the only way to fix the problem is by improving your own diet, health, wellness and stress levels.

Mainstream medicine relies on prescribed medications to suppress or relieve a symptom, putting a band-aid on it. This form of treatment will not work for a person who has pyrrole disorder. Unfortunately, sufferers of pyroluria fall through the cracks and are often misdiagnosed and given medication that can lead to further deterioration in health.

It can be so easily fixed, by getting your levels tested via a pyroluria or kryptopyrrole test, which is a simple urine test. Most naturopaths can get you a test, or a great doctor will also do it, if they have a good understanding of natural medicine. Once your results are in, your GP or naturopath will be able to prescribe you with individually tailored nutritional supplements that can be made up, specifically for your needs, at a chemist, and give you some dietary advice to rectify your body's underlying imbalances. BOOM! You're winning and hopefully not feeling as tired, stressed, depressed or hating the world anymore.

When I was under a tremendous amount of stress, due to a situation that was out of my control, at the time, I found myself diving deeper and deeper into the darkness. I was short-fused and short-tempered, feeling angry, lost, hopeless and saddened all at the same time. The slightest thing would cause my brain to snap, then explode—I even kicked a hole in the wall one night. This was not like me. I had never been an angry or negative person, so I knew something was wrong. I was eating healthily and exercising, but probably not sleeping enough and definitely not handling my stress levels well. I confided in a holistic GP, and told him I was losing my shit. Literally, I wanted to drive my car into a wall. He said five words that changed my life around. "Have you tested your pyroll?" When the results came back, they showed that my levels were off the charts. "No wonder you feel like a psycho," my doctor said. My zinc, magnesium and especially B vitamins were almost non-existent. I started taking my own individually tailored pyroll tablets, and within weeks felt my old self returning. My moods improved and I could handle the stress I was still enduring way better. I felt brighter and happier, like a fog had lifted. I couldn't thank my doctor enough for having that understanding of natural health and healing and not just resorting to prescribed and chemical-laden medication. This is my doctors quote "the body knows best; our job is to listen."

So please, if you are feeling low, anxious, depressed and unable to cope, then ask your parents if you can get this simple urine test FIRST to see what your natural body is up to and what your nutrient levels are doing. Doesn't it make sense to see what is happening on the inside first, rather than taking an unnecessary pill?

Then, if all of your "inside business" is working correctly, and you don't have pyroluria or you have checked off other sections in this book, seeking further help is definitely crucial. Just understand that your body works for you not against you. It tries its hardest 24/7, 365 days a year to rectify the wrongs and make them right.

So, when any health issue or mental health issue arises it is so important to ask why,

WINTER

AUTUMN

THE PERIOD CYCLE

SPRING

SUMMER

PERIODS

Miss red. Rags. Aunt flow. That time of the month. Lady business.

WTF – I CANT EVEN DEAL

Fellas, guys, male counterparts! This is not a cue to skip ahead. In fact, you really need to read this section if you want to understand why your girlfriend, sister or mum turns into a crazy, mad psycho at the drop of a hat some days. This section is full of important clues that will keep you out of harm's way or, more importantly, keep you branded the world's best boyfriend, sibling or son. Just by reading this section you will have been given the key that unlocks the door to the opposite sex, and you will be able to understand and decipher them much more easily. And girls, this is life. This explanation will give you the answers to why you can feel horrid one day and perfectly happy the next. WTF!

Now, I am not going to go into the scientific names and phases of the menstrual cycle. Rather, I am going to explain the hormonal rhythms and how they make us feel, emotionally, during certain phases of the 28-30-day cycle that every female has each month.

Your monthly cycle has four unique phases. Each one brings about different physical and emotional strengths and weaknesses. But first, let's look quickly over what each hormone brings to the table.

PERIODS

Meet ESTROGEN, the gorgeous party girl (when she is behaving and her levels are normal). She is the reason you are a woman. She helped make your boobs and bits, and she is the reason why you can have babies.

Estrogen increases the brain's serotonin, the hormone most associated with happiness. But, depending on the time of the month and the levels she wishes to give you or take away from you, she too can be a little bipolar, making you feel ecstatic one day and severely depressed the next.

Normal estrogen levels - great looking skin, smooth, shiny, lustrous hair, feeling sexy, vibrant and outgoing.

OUT OF WACK hormones look more like this:
High estrogen levels - can cause anxiety, irritability, heavy periods, sore boobs, weight gain, cellulite and can make you feel crap.

Low estrogen levels - can also make you feel like a pile of period poo: irregular periods, depressed, anxious, mood swings, panic attacks, F-ing hating the world and everyone in it.

Meet PROGESTERONE. When she is healthy she is Miss Calm, alleviating depression, reducing anxiety and promoting normal sleep patterns.

WTF – I CANT EVEN DEAL

Miss Calm also helps to regulate your cycle, but her main job is to get your uterus ready for pregnancy (don't forget that is why chicks have periods, after all). After you ovulate (release an egg, which wants to get fertilised to make a baby) each month, progesterone helps thicken the lining of the uterus in preparation for a fertilised egg. If there is no fertilised egg, progesterone levels drop again and you get your period.

Normal progesterone, or Miss Calm, does just what her name implies. She has a calming effect on your moods, similar to that of serotonin, a hormone that helps to enhance moods. So, when your periods are close by, and levels of progesterone and estrogen begin to DROP, this can cause the shit, sad and sorry feelings to re-emerge, which is totally normal, every month.

OUT OF WACK
High progesterone levels - fatigue, feeling low, depressed, tender boobs, mood swings, bloating, loss of libido and even a lost lust for life.

Low progesterone levels - may include weight gain, bloating, pimples, changes in appetite, muscle and joint pain, sleeplessness, irritability and difficulty concentrating.

PERIODS

Estrogen and progesterone are hormones that work together so if one is out of whack then the other will most likely be, also.

Meet TESTOSTERONE. He is a male sex hormone, but women actually need small amounts of testosterone, too, as part of the mix of hormones that keep mood, energy levels, sex drive and bodily functions working smoothly.

High testosterone - can mean you have too much of the boy hormones, so you have excess body hair (chin and upper lip in particular), missing or no periods, acne, oily skin, deepening of the voice and changes in body shape with increase in muscle mass.

Low testosterone - can mean lower energy, low mood, low sex drive and changes in sleep patterns.

So, girls if you feel shit, sad, sorry, up, down and every which way around, like you're on the dodgiest roller coaster ever, then one big factor could definitely be those crazy hormones. And as a growing, developing woman, it is wise to make sure all your hormone levels are tested, especially if you constantly feel these negative crazy emotions day in, day out.

Note: all teenagers, in fact all women, naturally

experience these feelings during certain days of their cycle. If your hormone levels are all balanced and working well, you won't have as much of a problem with excessive mood swings. But, if your emotions and moods are constantly low, out of whack, depressive and generally fu*#ed up, then before saying you are depressed, it would be wiser to get a blood test to have a look at what your hormones are doing and whether they are all working within healthy levels. While you are at it, get a urine test to check your pyroluria levels also.

You know what though? Feeling shit, sad, sorry, tired, irritated, angry, happy, excited, sexy, awesome, hating and loving life from day to day is NORMAL for every female, depending on where you are in your cycle and what your hormones are doing. So, let's dive a little deeper into this, because working alongside your cycle and understanding your cycle along with your corresponding emotions can make life a hell of a lot easier for you and everyone around you. Guess what, there is no ignoring this. You get a period every single month, so you may as well embrace that shit, or should I say blood!

Even if your hormones are functioning normally, you are still going to have ups and downs as your estrogen and progesterone levels rise and drop throughout your cycle.

PERIODS

Guys, this is the key that will unlock the girl mysteries, so listen up.

The easiest way to break this up is thinking about your 28-30-day cycle as seasons.

Each week, or so, has its very own season.

Winter = Bleeding. Days 1-7

Spring= Just after your period. Days 7-14

Summer = The middle of your cycle. Days 14-21

Autumn = The days leading up to your period. Days 21-30

WINTER. Days 1-7. The start of your period means your hormones, estrogen and progesterone, both take a nose dive into shitsville. The party girl, estrogen, is not feeling like partying, and Miss Calm (progesterone) has just turned into a sleepy sloth, so you are left with all the emotions. You feel pissed off at everything. Then you cry about feeling pissed off at everything. Then you're angry about crying and feeling pissed off at everything, and then you're just depressed, irritable, tired, and W H A T E V E R! Not to mention the cramps, aches, pains and headaches you get, because the emotional roller coaster isn't enough, right?

WTF – I CANT EVEN DEAL

So why is it called winter? Because all you want to do is withdraw and hibernate in your bedroom ALONE! You want to cover up and put a heat pack on your belly just like you would on a freezing cold winter's day. Having your period is not all bad though, there are positives. You have lots of creative energy, so painting, writing, vision boards, meditation and reading can all feel really good at this time, along with good, warming, wholesome, home-cooked "mum" food (without the mum annoying you, of course) and chocolate, lots of chocolate.

Tips to get you through this phase:

- Pull back on social media. It would have to be the worst time to be looking at a hot chick (who is in her summer) killing it at life, when here you are, feeling like a pus party just erupted on your face, bloated and depressed.

- Don't eat all the sugar. You are already tired and grumpy, and the sugar dump will just make you feel even worse in the long run.

- Tell your friends or boyfriend; it is nothing to be ashamed of. Let them know you have your period and either need some space or a little extra special care, cuddles and patience during this week.

PERIODS

- Don't worry. This will all pass and you will be feeling sooooo much better in a few days, come spring and summer. And just know, the self-doubt and destructive feelings you have from time to time are most likely just due to your hormonal changes. Keep a cycle journal and note down your feelings, aches and pains, irritations, energy levels and body changes each day. That way you will know what is coming around the corner.

SPRING days 7-14. Woohooo, your period has stopped and you start to feel better again as estrogen begins to rise. The party girl is slowly returning along with brighter skin, shiny hair and—got to love this—your body will be feeling the skinniest and sexiest it has all month. #feelingawesome.

Spring is finally here. Your energy has returned and you will want to get outside and socialise in a cute little dress. You will want to adventure, be spontaneous and have fun. It is a great time to do your homework or that assignment you have been putting off, because you will be feeling confident and self-assured. Remember, increased estrogen = happy. So if you are still feeling low and depressed, take a look at the other check list options in this book and perhaps get a blood test to see what your hormones are doing.

WTF - I CANT EVEN DEAL

Note: everyone is different and your body is still figuring itself out (you're young), so that is why it is so important to journal your daily feelings so you can refer back to a certain day of the month and a feeling associated with it.

SUMMER Days 14-21. How good is summer? Estrogen is the highest which means the party girl is rocking it, making you feel beautiful, sexy and energetic. You want to wear the shortest mini skirt you can find, and you are happy! You feel on the top of the world. People are magnetised to you and want to be you and be around you. You are now that hot girl on Instagram you were looking at in your winter.

You are Wonder Woman in this phase and can do it all: school work, socialising, sport. You can even take criticism with a grain of salt; nothing worries you. You feel like you are ticking all the boxes and winning at life. But beware, just like a hot summer's day, too much sun can deplete your energy and so too can this summer phase if you go too hard, because just around the corner is autumn and the slow descent back towards winter. Enjoy feeling fine now, but just be mindful about what is coming, and maybe take some time to forward-plan your diary, events and life for the emotional times ahead.

PERIODS

AUTUMN Days 21-28. Your body is getting ready to bleed again (if you're not pregnant). Progesterone is high, therefore you will be feeling a little fatigued, shit, sad and sorry, with sore boobs to top it off. And both estrogen and progesterone levels are about to drop into complete and utter shitsville again. It is in these autumn days, leading up to your period, that you can feel a little bipolar—up and down emotionally. One day you are feeling great and the next day you are snappy as hell. Your appetite increases and you want all the sugar and all the carbs, which makes you feel like a fat, bloated, swollen and zitty blob. FUN!

It is around these final days prior to your period that you may want to go within and shut out the world around you. You crave alone time, and your friends and boyfriend may start to annoy the hell out of you. The best thing to do is just that. Retreat, stay home, don't attend that weekend party, as you are most likely to get into an argument with your best friend and have a huge fight over nothing.

It is not really a great time for focusing your attention on anything. Don't be surprised if you flip out and feel like pressing delete on that assignment you have been working hard on for the last few weeks because you have read it back and it sounds like a fail. STOP. Don't do it; wait until your emotions are more rational, and

WTF - I CANT EVEN DEAL

just remember, you are only feeling this way because of your hormones. IT'S NORMAL, and soon you will understand why all these emotions are surfacing, because you are about to bleed in a week's time.

The important thing to remember in this week of your cycle is to listen to your body. If you don't feel like exercising or joining in on a social gathering or seeing your boyfriend every day, then don't. Explain to everyone you really just need some alone time and space because you are getting your period. It is really that easy.

As females, we always try to hide the fact that we are about to get our period, as though it's a bad, demonised, gross beast we don't want to know anything about. But guess what, every single woman on the planet goes through the same thing, every month. We need to change our perception on this topic so that it is something we can openly talk about with our girlfriends and boyfriends, instead of suffering alone in emotional silence. How nice would it be if you said to your boyfriend, "babe, I'm leading up to my period and you know I can get a little grumpy. Do you mind giving me some space or extra cuddles to make me feel better?" Instead of completely ignoring him and having him think you're a psycho for no reason. Explain to your friends, "if I'm snappy it is just

PERIODS

because I am about to get my period and I'm sorry in advance. I am just feeling tired." Problem sorted!

Remember, winter is next, which is almost a continuation of these feelings. So, go easy on yourself. The nicer you are to yourself and the more you respect and listen to your own needs and wants, the easier these shitty emotional weeks will be for you.

And the cycle starts again. Day 1, winter.

See it never stops. We continue to cycle around and around like a bicycle wheel. There is really no point in fighting it; instead, honour it and be proud of it. Understand each season and emotion and you will become so much more in-tune with your body and brain. A great thing to do is keep an emotional journal so you can look back on the previous days for guidance: "why do I feel like shit today and I'm in summer, day 15?" Look back at last month or the month prior and see what you wrote down in previous day 15s. You might be surprised; you were probably feeling the exact same way in the months that have passed.

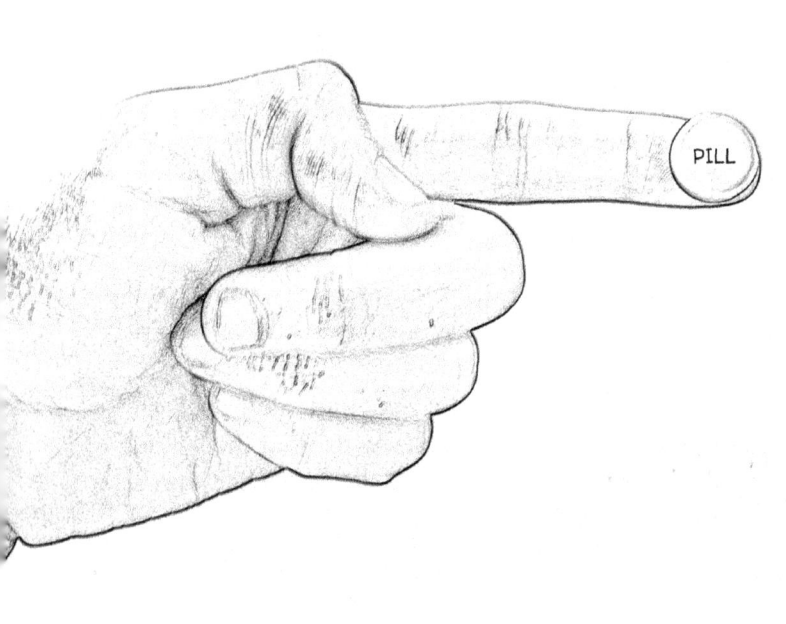

THE PILL

WTF - I CANT EVEN DEAL

I am not going to talk too much about the pill, an oral contraceptive, or little tablet, you are usually given in your teenage years as

a method for preventing pregnancy, or to help "fix" an issue you may be having, like acne or irregular, painful periods etc.

We are very lucky to have the pill as an option for birth control. But it is so important to do your research into this little tablet, as it pretty much just acts like a band-aid, covering up any abnormal issues you are having. These issues are things like acne or missed periods, and it dulls down your hormone levels so you can't fall pregnant, which can have some huge side effects. One of those side effects is the depletion of the available vitamins in your body and brain that keep you healthy and happy. The pill has been known to deplete the important B vitamins which help to convert serotonin, our happy hormone, and melatonin, our sleep hormone. This can disturb our sleep patterns and make us feel low, depressed and anxious. The pill can also possibly deplete our zinc and vitamin C levels which help to keep our immune system firing and healthy. This means we can become more prone to getting colds and flus. Unfortunately, the side effects don't stop there; because each and every woman is different, so too are the side effects. That is why taking some time to read about them with your mum or friends is really important.

If you are going to use the pill to help, or "band-aid", an issue like acne and irregular periods, chances are that when you eventually come off the pill, those issues will still be there. I myself have had this exact problem. I got my period when I was 15, then went on the pill when I was 16 because I had pimples. Little did I know, back then I only had bad skin because my hormones were a little out of whack and still working themselves out, as I had only had a handful of periods in that first year. My body just needed time and some extra care and attention. Instead, I ignored the signs (acne) and put a band-aid over it: the pill. It did fix my skin at the time; however, after taking the pill for 18 years and then not wanting to be on it anymore, all of those issues I had when I was 16 resurfaced and my acne came back at age 35 (WTF). It is only now in my late 30s that I wish I had listened to my body and sorted out my hormonal issues when I was 16 instead of ignoring them. My advice to you is make sure you understand your body's own natural period cycle, emotions and feelings attached to each stage of your cycle for a few years before, and if, you decide to go on the pill. Make sure you fix what is wrong first, before covering it up and having to fix it later on down the track. Get a blood test and make sure everything is normal prior to taking the pill, and if you are just taking the pill to not have a baby, don't forget the pill does not protect against STDs!

Just remember, feeling all the crazy emotions is quite normal, depending on your monthly cycle.

GUS

WTF - I CANT EVEN DEAL

Ok guys, the following hormones relate to you!

TESTOSTERONE. What is it? In simple terms, it makes your balls and makes you ballsy.

Testosterone is a hormone found in both females and males; however, guys have much higher levels of testosterone than chicks. That's why they are guys. Testosterone helps maintain a number of important bodily functions in dudes, including: sex drive, sperm production, muscle mass and strength, fat distribution, bone density and blood cell production. Because testosterone affects so many functions in the body, it's differentiating levels can bring about significant physical and emotional changes and challenges in growing teens.

Normal testosterone levels will make you feel GOOD, confident, motivated and energetic. You have greater strength and muscle mass, and your body fat is usually lower than girls'. Your sex drive is also likely to be much higher than your girlfriend's. Key thing to remember is you are still young and your body's levels are still working themselves out. And this is where the tinge of crazy psycho can come sneaking in.

GUYS

Around age 14, testosterone levels hit a peak, resulting in a possible growth spurt. This is the kind of growth spurt where your arms and legs feel way too long for your body and you feel kind of dorky, goofy and uncoordinated. That is just because your nervous system has also had to rewire itself to keep up—meaning you might be inclined to trip over your huge, growing, hairy hobbit feet until your body kind of figures out what is normal for it.

Can you have too much of this male ego-boosting hormone? Yes; it can cause pimples, excessive facial and body hair, a big Adam's apple and a deeper voice. You may also be more reckless, aggressive and angry.

Whereas, LOW testosterone can lead to feelings of sadness and depression, poor memory and concentration and a lack of motivation and self-confidence. Not to mention fatigue, increased body fat, low sex-drive, acting like an ass and generally not loving life at all.

As a growing teenager, your hormone levels are going to fluctuate. In fact, there are around two years of ups and downs when you hit puberty: mood swings, pimples, stinky body odour, voice changes and awkwardness. Then after the puberty years are out of the way, your body will be fully developed and the hormones will even out to a steady production of testosterone, making you feel less shit and more star quarterback.

How to deal

You are going to not want to talk some days, to retreat inwards and not be social with anyone, and this is totally normal. On other days, you are going to want to engage in anything to do with highly stimulating experiences like sex, drugs, loud music concerts, fast cars, risk-taking behaviour, school yard fights and adventure. Just knowing that these feelings are normal is the best course of action. Acting on these experiences is your call, but it might mean unnecessary trouble, suspension or being grounded by your parents. Know your limits!

Don't watch all the porn and become creepy. Instead, enjoy these increasing sexual feelings privately or with your girlfriend. That's what long showers are for.

Talk to your mates; they too are going through the exact same emotions and feelings that you are. The age-old bullshit saying that men don't share their feelings is long gone. It's the 21 century, and today's new motto is "it ain't weak to speak" thanks to the successful charity livin'.

GUYS

Go and expel some of that pent-up energy playing sport, or take it out on a punching bag instead of your sister.

And don't be so hard on yourself. All these crazy roller coaster feelings are NORMAL. Go and read the girls' period section and you will be soon saying "thank gosh I'm a guy."

Emotions, crappy days, feeling shit, sad and sorry is totally normal every now and then. It is only when these days turn into months upon months, or years, without feeling any better about life that you need to be concerned. That is what this book is here for: a checklist of emotions. "Why am I feeling like this and is this normal?" Most likely, the answer is yes.

WTF – I CANT EVEN DEAL

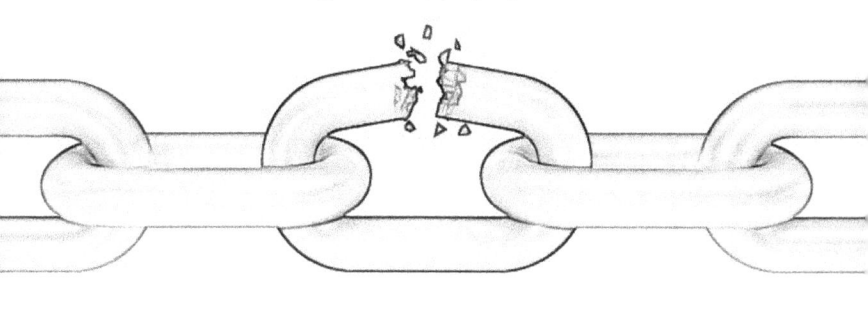

WTF - I CANT EVEN DEAL

The teenage years are definitely the most exciting and fun, yet they are also the most challenging, dramatic and stressful times of our lives. It is a time in your life when you are supposed to figure out the next chapter, beyond high school and into university or the work force. You have to figure out who you are, who you like, what you like, what you don't like. You also have to discover what you are good at and what you want to do with the rest of your life, not to mention trying to figure out your own crazy emotions. Then you're also trying to find out how to please everyone, how to stay out of trouble, how to get As, all while looking good, being available 24/7 on social media and staying healthy and happy all the time—brain-friggen-strain!

The pressures can be damn right overwhelming
- peer pressure
- parent pressure
- popularity pressure
- appearance pressure
- relationship pressure
- future pressure
- culture pressures.

BRAIN STRAIN

Just getting out of bed in the morning is a real struggle, let alone all the other added stuff. No wonder you feel stressed, anxious and overwhelmed from time to time.

Unfortunately, today's society has also made it impossible for you to escape your problems; the internet realm constantly keeps you alerted to the world's problems, everyone else's problems and your own problems, all at the same time.

When I was 14 and had a bad day at school, I couldn't wait to get home. I'd play in the pool or watch mindless TV for a couple of hours before having dinner, playing with my dog and going to bed. Waking up to a new day didn't seem so bad.

Now, you cannot escape the BAD. A bad day at school usually means it sprawls out over social media, or a bombardment of texts. So, when you are home you cannot disconnect unless you know how to do it.

Do you know how to disconnect from the BAD? Most likely not, because how teenagers zone out and relax in this day and age is via social media. Thanks to your phones, your generation has been employed as the front line (In army terms that means the military forefront that is closest to the action).

WTF – I CANT EVEN DEAL

You are the front line to the world's emotions, first handedly filtering through a continuous flow of questions, information, emotions, events, issues, human behaviour and trauma as it happens, instantaneously. You, my friend, are not getting paid very much to decipher the problems of the world and everyone in it, are you? In fact, you are being rorted with these unexplainable and overwhelming feelings of pressure, anxiety and depression, and no wonder why. See, if you are going to be this front line social media "soldier", at least you can have your say as to what sort of army you want to join or follow.

Have you ever heard of "your vibe attracts your tribe"? Or have you ever seen a clip on social media where one person randomly starts laughing on a train, uncontrollably, and before long the whole train is laughing along, but no one actually knows what they're laughing about?

We humans work with ENERGY, good or bad. We feel it and we respond to it. Most of the time we do so subconsciously. So why subject yourself and your energy field to negative, useless shit that is only going to make you feel low and unfulfilled, stressed and anxious? These are things like negative social media pages, hateful social situations or unnecessary daily pressures. Instead, cut out anything that doesn't give you a positive feeling. If something makes you feel bad, sad, sick, hurt or angry all the time, it is ultimately filling you up with negative energy, which your body, and especially your over-stimulated brain, cannot function or deal with. You may as well invite, with open arms, issues like depression, sickness, fatigue and unhappiness in the front door, willingly.

Let's fix this problem right now. How can you feel good more often?

Surround yourself with positive energy and good vibes as much as you can.

- Being around like-minded, happy, positive people and situations will boost your spirits. You will catch their vibes and it will make you feel good too.

- Fresh air and nature is an unlimited source of positive energy. Just think how great you feel after a walk in the fresh air, a swim in the ocean or when you are sitting under the shade of a tree with your feet on the grass (p.s not looking at your phone while doing it). You feel re-energised, happier and are more at ease.

- Exercise helps detoxify negative energy in your body and pressure in your head, helping to release the feel-good hormones that make you feel instantly happier, healthier and more alive.

- Healthy food also carries a good/happy energy which makes your brain and body feel good.

What should you be staying away from, energy-wise? Or, what carries a negative mojo? The type of energy you feel when there is a big fight and someone is lying unconscious on the ground (the "oh shit!" feeling).

- News channels and social media. How often are there happy stories on the news? Not often, and the same goes with social media, as we tend to negatively compare ourselves with others.

- Negative people will make your energy shrivel up and your heart beat faster, which will make you feel anxious, upset and angry, all at the same time.

- Cigarettes, drugs and alcohol initially release small amounts of feel-good hormones before dumping a bombardment of crappy emotions and hormones into your bloodstream. This makes you feel horrible and it is why you feel like another smoke or drink. It is a vicious cycle you will constantly be trying to combat.

- Fake light and too much screen time shrinks your pineal gland, the control centre of happiness in your brain, shutting down your emotions so you become a scroll zombie.

There are plenty more, like hating on yourself, being judgemental towards yourself and others, stress, not moving your body and eating unhealthy, processed foods which we will get into later.

I know you can't exactly cut out all negative energy or situations in your life, like the moody bus driver, your assignments, or school (if they are some negative issues you deal with). But if you are not getting attacked from every angle, like school, home, friends, and alone time, it will make the pressures you face a little easier to deal with.

One of the big issues you guys are facing, which is a huge contributing factor towards making you feel shit, sad and sorry, is the explosion of pressures from every single area of your life: parent pressure, culture pressure, relationship pressures. There are so many pressures teens are faced with daily and everyone wants a little slice of your pie. If you don't know how to portion-control that pie it will all be eaten up, leaving you depleted and starving, mentally.

WTF – I CANT EVEN DEAL

How can you deal with these overwhelming pressures and keep some pie for yourself?

You need to find an escape from life and its daily pressures, or a bunker to retreat to. You need to find a bunker and have that space filled with the ingredients in which you can make more pie, figuratively speaking. I'm talking about a feel-good spot where you can mentally escape, whether that be by reading comics, playing sport, painting, singing, writing, drawing or walking the dog. You need to find whatever it is that makes you feel alive, deep inside of you, whatever makes you smile when you are all ALONE. You need to find that thing YOU want to do without needing to document it, photograph it or capture it to prove your self-worth to someone else. Ask yourself, am I doing this for me or for the satisfaction of others on social media, just for the possible "likes"? What do I really enjoy doing? What is that one thing that always makes me happy and smiling at myself? What is it? Once you have it, write it down. That, my friend, is your bunker, your ammunition that will reload your feel-good endorphins and help you cope with life's daily pressures.

Think of your brain as a roof gutter. The clearer it is the easier the water can flow out of it. The more leaves that fall, or in your case the more stuff you add into your brain that doesn't need to be there, the more the

BRAIN STRAIN

gutter will become clogged. This makes the run-off harder and harder, until the gutter eventually overflows and you're drowning, having a mental breakdown, stressed, emotional and can't deal. You have CLOGGED up the flow of thought processes in your brain because you haven't taken the time to sweep away and unclog the build-up of old, unnecessary leaves and crap that don't need to be there. You can easily blow away the leaves each day by doing something that makes your brain feel good. Remember, your brain actually doesn't feel good when it stares at a screen. You need to learn to physically and mentally release the pressures of the day by doing something which makes you feel good. Even if it is nothing but closing your eyes and listening to music for 30 minutes without being attached to your phone, your homework, your friends, your parents, your girl or boyfriend or the stressors that blew the storm of leaves in and clogged that shit up in the first place. You will know when your gutter is starting to feel full and the flow is slowing down. Your body will slow down and feel sloth-like, all drooped down and hunched over. Your eyes blink less and stare more. You feel anxious, stressed, tired, overwhelmed, nervous, sad, shit and sorry… Time to get the leaf blower out and blast those feelings away. Time to look at what has taken over or closed-up your gutter and brain to the point of mental overflow. What is it too much of? And too little of?

WTF – I CANT EVEN DEAL

The best way to escape your pressures is to switch them off inside your own brain. We are so lucky to be able to close our eyes and be, think, do or have whatever we want, just by thinking and imagining it! Your thoughts are free to wonder; they are the one thing that no matter what is going on outside of you, they never have to be restricted to a situation or your body's small space. No one can ever read your thoughts or take them away if you don't allow them to. Your powerful thoughts can travel through space and time. Close your eyes and you could be sitting on a camel in the Sahara Desert! No, scrap that, close your eyes and you could be riding on a lion's back through the Sahara Desert. A prisoner is only imprisoned in the physical state. But close your eyes and your imagination and thoughts can have you sitting at a restaurant eating a five course meal in Paris. Break out of the prison in your brain. Give your thoughts free range beyond your body's tiny space. You have the entire universe to explore, if you want to.

How do you break out? For starters, get out of lock mode. Cure yourself of phone-to-face syndrome.

Have you ever wondered why circus elephants don't just run away? They are that big and powerful, they could easily trample the tent down and run away from captivity.

BRAIN STRAIN

Well, from birth, some elephants are chained around one leg so they are unable to move beyond a small space. As time goes on, the elephant grows up bigger and stronger and could easily break that chain off. But because, from such a young age, the elephant has been taught to believe it is physically captive, it continues to feel captive, mentally. Once the elephant's brain has been brainwashed to believe the chain on its leg means it is tied up, the handlers let the elephant wonder around FREE, with the chain not secured, just tied onto its leg. So, even though the elephants are free, they still think they cannot go anywhere. Even these huge and incredibly strong animals can become imprisoned, mentally, by the smallest of things; that is how powerful our thoughts are.

You have the ability to change your thoughts; they can, and will, change your life. You just have to believe and learn that it is possible and easily done.

Do you think there is much of a difference between the elephant's chain and your phone? They both keep you in a confined space, not moving. They both, in a way, imprison your brain and thoughts, taking them away from the outside world. They both teach the brain to be numb, stop thinking and become oblivious to what life should really be about. You are allowing your thoughts to become less and less powerful by taking away their ability to flow freely, like an elephant in the wild. You can look at a flower on a screen, but it won't give your body the intense energy, emotions, senses, feelings or any human growth or expansion as it would if you touched, smelt, looked into or felt a real flower. The more desensitised your brain becomes, the more you invite a depressive state into your daily life. Depressive, means to be in low spirits from loss or detachment of your senses, leaving you in a sad and depressed state.

You might be feeling things like, "I am so unhappy," "I am so depressed," or "I can't," when, in fact, that is just your thought pattern (like the chained elephant). But guess what, YOU can change your thoughts. "I am happy, I am getting happier every day and I can do this."

What I am trying to say is, if you become stuck thinking in a confined way due to stress or pressures overtaking your life, it usually means you haven't taken time out to unclog those leaves that stop your brain flowing freely.

How to UNCLOG the brain strain?

Like I said, find your bunker and retreat into it with whatever it is that makes you feel good, happy, refreshed and reenergised, if not once a day, at least once a week.

BRAIN STRAIN

- *Get off your phone* and learn to expand your brain and intellectual capacity beyond a screen.

- Meditate or imagine, these are both incredible ways to expand and grow your brain and thought capacity. If you think of your brain as a muscle, you will want to make it as strong and powerful as possible. This is the perfect way to do it: close your eyes and take ten deep, slow breaths. Then let your thoughts wander; take yourself on a journey across the world, under the sea, wherever you want to go. The world is yours for the taking when you close your eyes and get lost in it. Why do you think toddlers and young kids are always so happy and filled with positive energy? Because they are in a constant state of fun and imagination. There are no leaves in their brains, just leaves to play with.

- Go interact with other humans, face to face. Talk more, laugh and enjoy people's company away from a screen relationship. We are losing this ability at an alarming rate. Walk down the road and smile at strangers instead of walking down the road looking at your phone. As important as it is to learn to be alone without the distraction of devices, it is equally as important to learn how to be with people without the distraction of devices also.

- Get moving. When you move your body it actually helps to move stagnant energy and declutter thought patterns in your brain. It acts like your leaf blower, clearing unwanted crap out of your body and brain.

Here are some other great exercises to help with BRAIN STRAIN, anxiety, panic attacks and stress.

Next time you're stressed, anxious and cannot breathe, step outside barefoot if you can or even look out the window of your class room. Try and look for a tree, even if it's far away. Now find ONE leaf buried deep in that tree and focus all your attention on that one leaf. Look at it and take it in, because you are probably the only person in the ENTIRE WORLD who has ever noticed that one tiny leaf.

Who else would have ever taken time out of their day to stare and appreciate that one leaf on the tree before you? No-one. They may have looked at the whole tree in a quick glance but never looked deep enough at that one individual leaf.

Appreciate it! You can own that special moment and that tiny part of the universe that only you have noticed, acknowledged and seen. By creating that particular moment in time, you will bring a calm

BRAIN STRAIN

stillness to your mind and body and be able to turn your day around in that instant, breathing easier.

Here is another great exercise to do when you're stressed or anxious, on the verge of a panic attack. Your brain is less likely to have a panic attack while it is concentrating on form, so to really mix it up and shift your focus, try and count numbers out of order. When you feel as though you are going to have a panic attack start counting 1, 2, 3, 8, 6, 12, 11, 15. It's important to count out of order to trick your brain. It is a trick I used to do with all my patients when I was a paramedic.

IN CONCLUSION, DON'T STRAIN YOUR BRAIN. It is the only one you have. Instead, become the master of it. When it makes you feel anxious, depressed, low and slow, it is giving you a hint that something is off balance and needs attention in your life. Whether it is too much pressure, too much bad food, too much partying or too much of everything, listen to what it needs to declutter. Give it some attention, real life, love, growth and reality—not fake screen-reality.

Change your thoughts to change your life. Be the powerful wild elephant, not the captive meek one.

SOCIAL MEDIA

WTF - I CANT EVEN DEAL

This social media thing is a full time job. Why? Because we are always connected, always on and always checking our phones for FOMO (fear of missing out). This constant ON mode is time consuming, damn right exhausting and, well, a little anti-social, as, after all, it is based in a virtual reality not the actual, real world.

But we all do it because it has become second nature for us to check online and scroll around "mindlessly" when we are waiting on the bus, in a cue, or anytime we are not engaged in doing something with our minds or hands.

We feel as though we have to fill up those unattended seconds and minutes of our lives, when we used to kind of just stare off into space and dream. And this is where the problems start, because we are choosing to swap real life with online life, and our lifetime with wasting time. WHY are we doing this?

It has become a habit, an addictive practice and routine.

"Bing", a message or notification sounds off on your phone and triggers your brain, instantly, to think, "oh! What is that? I must respond and see asap."

SOCIAL MEDIA

You are responding straight away because that "bing" noise is the reward, a pleasing invitation that tells your brain you have friends, likes, someone interested in what you're doing, and it feels good. The feel-good section in your brain just lit up, exploding and sending those feel-good emotions all around your body. How can you ignore this feel-good "bing" and not respond straight away? It is almost impossible, and therefore it becomes a normalised pattern and habit every single time you hear or see your phone. It is ADDICTIVE because you want to feel more of those good, approval-seeking feelings from others telling you you're awesome, engaging in your life or your posts. So, like an addiction you want more and more and more. You therefore post more and spend more time on social media, chasing rewards or self-approval from others because it feels good and it makes YOU feel like a better person.

When you have an itch on your foot, your brain says scratch it. When you need to pee, you go to the toilet. When you look at your phone, your brain says look at it. It has become a normal, everyday part of our lives, a habit that can be very destructive, dangerous and one that is a huge contributing factor to making you feel shit, sad and sorry.

What happens when you post a photo, send a text

message or update your Facebook and nothing comes back, no response, no likes, no love? We keep checking and checking and checking, and when there is no reward it sends negative messages to the brain, invoking feelings of self-doubt, sadness, loneliness and a kick in the guts: "what is wrong with me?" "Why does no-one like me?" "What am I doing wrong?" When in fact, it is probably just a slow time of the day and no-one is on social media at that time, or they saw it and are too busy to respond. Physiologically it has left you feeling f_#ked up, in mental overdrive, over analysing everything in those seconds until you finally get a response which perks you up again. It is a vicious cycle that will continue as long as you are interacting with the power of your phone.

Then there is COMPARISON, another normal human habit that can be magnified tenfold due to social media. We all know people only post the best pics, the funniest moments and the posts that are most likely going to get a better response or more likes. We want others to say good things to us, not bad. We want to hear, "you're so pretty," "you're so lucky," "you're so fit." This makes us feel good (remember that feel-good "bing"). No-one wants to see a photo of someone crying and unhappy with snot running out of their nose because they just failed an exam, unless it is someone hugely famous or popular because

SOCIAL MEDIA

then it would make little, normal us feel better about ourselves. That would make Facebook and Instagram pretty miserable, seeing sad, negative posts constantly.

Being on any form of social media is going to make you compare your life with the lives of others, as hard as you try not to, it is just human nature. "How come they are always so happy?" "Why do they get to wear the best clothes all the time?" "Why is she so pretty?" "Why is he so fit?" When we compare, we feel envious, crap, sad, anxious and depressed because our lives don't match up or are not as good.

Understanding that social media is not reality is so important. A photo is not real life. It could have been taken months ago; it might have been photoshopped or said it was taken on a beach in Hawaii, when it was actually taken under a palm tree at a local park. Words on a screen are just that—words. You can either believe what you are reading or have some understanding that there are no rules governing a screen or photo. Whatever goes, goes, and you are never going to know the truth unless you, yourself, are the one posting it.

The best thing to do is find real, authentic people you enjoy following that don't bring out your negative self-talk. Unfollow the fake. You know who they are and how their page makes you get all uncomfortable, fidgety and bitchy. What are you going to gain by following people who make you feel like you are less than or low? Nothing, just unfollow.

FACTS

Did you know too much screen time can disturb sleep quality and how much sleep you get? Sleep makes you feel good, mentally and physically, and is super important for growing teenagers. So if you are not getting enough, due to hours of scrolling, you're going to be tired, grumpy, unsatisfied and more emotional.

If you find yourself waking up in the middle of the night and checking your social media, or if your phone is the very last thing you look at before you close your eyes at night and the very first thing you look at before you have had a chance to really open your eyes in the morning, then it is definitely time to set some boundaries. When you wake up in the morning, why would checking into someone else's life and day be more important than starting your day? It is kind of insulting to your life when you wake up and look at someone else's life before acknowledging your own, don't you think? You are putting it out there that your life isn't that important. Instead, wake up, GET UP, go look outside and take in YOUR day, YOUR life, before touching your phone. By just doing this one simple thing you are empowering yourself and setting your own intellectual, emotional and mental standards for the day, instead of being a mindless scroll-zombie from the get go.

The more screen time, the more depressed you feel—FACT, and a proven fact at that.

- Staying still for too long slows down the energy systems in your body making your brain and body feel slow, sad and sluggish.

- Staring into a fake light or screen reduces the size of your pineal gland. This tiny organ regulates your daily rhythms (when you feel sleepy and alert), how you are feeling mentally and emotionally, your hormone levels, stress levels and physical performance. The pineal gland is that GUT feeling or that connection to your real self or soul—YOU, what makes you, you. When it is preforming at optimal levels we feel amazing. When we shrink it by being on our phones for too long, being cooped up inside, not getting enough sunlight into our eyes, we lose our sense of self and feel lost.

- It is unsatisfying to mindlessly scroll and not actually learn or gain anything from it. For example, you can stare at a photo of a tree or you can actually look at a real live tree. There is no comparison; REAL LIFE will always make you feel better and more connected, engaged and alive.

- The more social media you engage with, the more disengaged you become with everything real: friendships, family and feelings. And this makes you feel alone. You may have 100,000 followers, but you may also feel like the loneliest person in the world because followers don't compare to the genuine interaction, conversation, expression and emotions that you experience and feel when you are talking to someone, face to face. Reading a text that says, "I love you" just doesn't compare to someone looking you in the eyes and saying, "I love you!"

- Always being ON and never disconnecting fully means you're placing huge pressure and stress on yourself to constantly respond and reply instantaneously. You do this for fear of missing out or fear that someone might unfollow you. This fear causes anxiety, depression and burnout, both mentally and physically. We are not designed to work 24/7, 365 days a year. Never switching off will break you down in all aspects of your mind and body. The more 'on' you are, the more unbalanced you will become.

SOCIAL MEDIA

OK, we get it. Too much social media is bad, so how can we BALANCE this addiction so it stops us feeling shit, sad and sorry?

- Set yourself daily limits. Only allow yourself to be on your phone certain times of the day, for certain time frames. Set your alarm for 30 minutes. Once that alarm goes off it's time to switch off.

- BREAK THE HABIT. Don't pick up your phone when you have nothing else to do or when you do have a spare second. Instead look around at life. Don't miss the butterfly sitting beside you because you have your head stuck in your phone. Don't waste your seconds and minutes on your phone. On average a teenager is on their phone 4+ hours a day. That is 28 hours a week and 112 hours a month, which means you have lost 56 days a year, or over two months a year, wasting your life looking at a screen. How long do you spend on your phone? Work it out. That is your lifetime.

- Social media can be great, but choose wisely where and what to spend your time on and what to engage with. You want to be using your time to spread happiness or as a tool for growing—growing your business or growing your brain with positivity, insight and knowledge. Decipher what is depleting your energy levels. For example, if you are on Instagram and that mean voice starts nagging in the back of your mind, that is going to start depleting your energy and clogging your gutter or brain. Choose two platforms like Facebook and Instagram or Snapchat and Facebook, and get rid of the rest. The people who want to follow you will follow you on those accounts.

- Have a technology detox. Every now and then give yourself an entire week off social media, or if that is too hard, at least an entire day without checking your social media or being on your phone. It will feel horrible at first, like breaking an addiction, but then it will feel awesome and will increase your energy levels, your moods and self-worth because there is no bullying, no pressure, no anything when you're not connected.

- Switch off your notifications. That way you won't constantly be reaching for your phone when you hear that "bing." Rather, set aside five minutes here and there throughout the day to check updates, comments and likes from a recent post, and chillax instead of being tense and alert all the time. If someone comments or likes a post you did, there is no need to reply asap. In fact, it

SOCIAL MEDIA

makes it look like all you do is sit on your phone. Make them think you are busy and have more important things to do... reply later.

If you feel shit, sad and sorry, then how much of your lifetime do you spend on this constricting device, ignoring the real world evolving around you? Try a little experiment. One day give yourself permission to spend as much time as you want, plus more, on your phone, in lala screen land. At the end of the day write down how you are feeling. Be honest! Accomplished? Happy? Fulfilled? Connected? Or perhaps tired? Low, slow, depressed, bored? Anxious?

Now, on another day make plans without your phone, leave it at home. Go to the beach, immerse yourself in laughter, nature, food, good energy and friends and at the end of the day write down how you feel.

This should give you a true indicator of the impact screen time has on your energy and emotions. And will let you know whether or not it is contributing to you feeling depressed, sad and shit.

RELATIONSHIPS

WTF - I CANT EVEN DEAL

I am only going to say a couple of things about this topic. If your relationship is making you feel shit, sad and sorry, it is not meant to be! Full stop.

It is natural for us to want to give so much of ourselves to someone we like or love in the hopes they will return the favour and love us back. We human beings crave love, attention and affection from someone or something, whether that be our boy or girl friends, pets, parents or friends. But what we are hopeless at is receiving love from ourselves. If we want love so badly from others, we also have to learn how to love ourselves. Without self-love, self-happiness, self-appreciation and knowing ourselves and who we really are first, how can we expect others to love us in the right way?

The more love and respect you have for yourself, the more love and respect you will receive from others.

One thing that you will constantly be learning about for the rest of your life is RELATIONSHIPS, because no two people are the same. No two people think the same, believe the same, see the same, hear the same or

RELATIONSHIPS

are the same. So, being so closely in a relationship or unity with someone else will always bring up issues. You may be looking at the blue sky and your partner may be looking at the grey clouds in the blue sky. These differences mean there will be heartache and disagreements, tears and triumphs, and this is with any relationship, not just boyfriends and girlfriends, but friends and family too.

If you understand one thing, know this: each person comes into your life for a reason. Usually it is to teach you something about yourself, and most likely that something will better you in the long run, even though it may feel like your world is ending if you break up with your partner or have a fight with your friend today.

Someone who will always be there for you, is you. So, take time to get to know the real you. Date you! Enjoy spending time with yourself and understand that you, first and foremost, will always have your own back. It is when you give up on yourself that life can really seem like a shitty place to be. The more you work on and love yourself, in a positive way, the more love you will have and bring into your world.

The best way to explain it is a boomerang. No, not the boomerang app on your phone, an actual boomerang you throw and it circles out in the atmosphere and comes back to you. Well, what you say and think and do does just that; it circles out into the atmosphere and comes back to you. If you are negative, hateful, bitchy, rude and mean, that is exactly what you invite back into your life. That is the energy you are sending out, and that is the energy you will get back like a slap in the face.

If you are genuine, kind, friendly, loving, happy, positive and fun, that is what your boomerang energy will come back to you with.

Ever heard the sayings:
"The more you give the more you get."
"What goes around comes around."
"You get what you think about."
"Don't do the crime if you can't do the time."
"You made your bed now you have to lie in it."

It all means the same thing. If you start working on yourself first, loving yourself and who you are as a person first, that is exactly what you invite others to do.

So, let me finish with what I started with. If your relationship is making you feel shit, sad and sorry, it is not meant to be! If you have lost who you really are as

RELATIONSHIPS

a person due to your relationship and putting everyone else's needs first, you need to flip the coin and start putting yourself first. Date yourself again.

If you feel like no one loves you, do you love yourself?

If people step all over you and mistreat you, do you mistreat and belittle yourself?

FOOD

WTF - I CANT EVEN DEAL

We all know teenagers can EAT, but did you know the foods you eat may be making you sad, depressed and feel like a crap?

We have all heard the saying "you are what you eat," but it actually is true. What your moods show on the outside is a direct reflection of what your body is doing on the inside. And because we have to eat every day to keep us going, like fuel on the fire, the food you eat also fuels your moods.

We have all been told to eat healthy, good nutritious food, bla bla bla. But here is why.

Food carries its very own positive or negative energy or viberation, depending on what it is. Foods that make us feel happy, positive and work well and naturally with our bodies are foods that carry a high energy. What are they? Any foods that haven't been manipulated or disturbed by man. Food that has naturally grown from the earth's soil, the sun's warmth and has been nourished by the sky's water is the food that contains the highest energy because it comes from the earth's GOODNESS.

FOOD

What foods could grow without man? Fruit, vegetables, nuts, seeds and grains. These foods have been around since day one, in every story you were taught and whichever one you may believe in today. Adam and Eve ate an apple; the dinosaurs grazed on grains and berries; or cave men hunted and gathered fruits from the trees. Long before you and I existed these foods have been flourishing naturally from the earth's core, soaking up all the essential minerals and nutrients from the soil, the sun and the rain.

Human bodies naturally match in energy to these foods. It's like a dog to a bone, like the sun and the moon, like fuel to the fire. And that is exactly what they can do for your body: fuel your body up so it can be the best functioning engine it could possibly be.

This is why our diets should be mostly made up of these foods, if we want to feel, think and live the best we can.

Society says we have become lazy and that is why we choose to open a packet of chips over eating healthily. But eating an apple actually requires less effort then opening a packet of chips because there is no packaging. There is no untwisting or cooking or microwaving fruit and veggies; you can just grab them in your hand and start eating.

WTF - I CANT EVEN DEAL

"But I feel hungrier two minutes after eating a banana or a carrot or any piece of fruit or veg" I hear you say. That is because it has gone into your body and within minutes of eating it, it has been devoured by every cell structure in your body like piranhas attacking flesh! Your body needed all the nutrients, minerals and goodness so badly, it is asking for more. You should be like, "yes, that's how fast my metabolism works when I feed it the good stuff." And what is even better is you can eat as much of it as you like without it doing any harm to your body, unlike ten pizzas a day would.

Fruits, vegetables, nuts, seeds, berries and healthy grains want you to eat them so they can throw a happy party inside of your gut and send positive vibes to your brain and butt—yes butt—because your bowels and intestine will be in cruise mode and not sluggish, fat, bloated mode like they would if you just ate a pizza.

Your brain will be charged with positive energy, because we eat to fuel our brain, the control centre of our bodies. It will be thinking lighter, clearer and sharper because it doesn't have to waste time counselling the sad sluggish liver to produce more bile, or encourage the bowels to work harder to get rid of the waste. It also won't need to delegate, navigate, instigate and motivate every functioning cell and organ in your body like it has to every day you put unhealthy crap into your body. So, you see, the more unhealthy food you eat, the more the brain is on alert mode and overworked to maintain the body, which leaves little time for the brain to think straight, let alone think happy, clear energetic thoughts. It is just thinking "farrrrk I'm tired, I'm sluggish, I'm over worked, exhausted, cloudy, slow, low and depressed because that is how every organ is feeling working overtime in this junk-riddled body of mine."

Opposed to that, healthy food allows the brain to almost switch off and be on holiday mode, because it knows each organ and cell needs and uses up the nutrients and minerals from the good food. It can relax and take a back seat, as it doesn't have to delegate or send out extra healing energy. The brain says "YES, I can finally have some time to think and think without these negative overworked feelings holding me back. I can think clearer and sharper and I can send off more energy to run and play and laugh, finally."

So right now, think about your moods. Are you low, sad, tired, depressed, irritated or shit, sad or sorry? If yes perhaps ask yourself what you have been eating. Is it foods that make your body work overtime shifts to digest it? Is it foods that make your body scream "WTF is this man-made packet junk and how am I meant to pull any nutrients out of this to fuel my brain and run my body effectively?"

WTF - I CANT EVEN DEAL

See, the man-made foods carry negative energy, or energetic frequencies, like a bad radio station not tuned in correctly, that makes the body feel negative. Eating foods that have preservatives, colouring, flavours, additives and numbers, is like sticking Coca-Cola into your car and using it as petrol, hoping it will drive you around. It may work for a kilometre or short period of time before conking out and corroding your engine altogether. Your body can't communicate with these man-made foods. It tries really hard but not without consequence.

Food that has a six-month to one-year shelf life, like all the food you see in the middle isles of the supermarket, is designed that way so it won't go off. If it can remain in this perfect, non-decomposing form for a year or more, imagine what your precious insides have to do to break that down. Once consumed, your body pretty much says, "WOW! I can't pull out any nutritional value from this because I don't know what this is or where it comes from. I'll just try and get the fat and sugar from it and store that for later because at least I can semi run off that for now until I get more food that is hopefully better than this. Then I have to try and digest this "food" which is going to take up every ounce of my energy because this is going to take days to digest. And hey, you out there who just ate this crap, sorry to say, but you are going to be left feeling fatigued, foggy, sluggish, slow, fat, bloated, sad and negative."

Now, what do you think happens when you continue to eat this negative-energy food, this processed, long shelf life, packet, man-made food for days, weeks and years consistently, when on the first day your body struggled to sort it out or digest it?

It continues to build up, struggle and back up, using all your energy to digest it.

You have just employed your body and gut to work overtime, day and night, for years without ever giving it a holiday or break. Of course, it's going to break down and you are going to get sick, depressed, diseased and become overweight because your body was not designed for these fake, man-made foods, day in, day out.

So, when you get sick, that is your body telling you it needs a break to heal on the inside. That is why you don't feel like eating anything when you are sick, because you physically can't deal with the food inside your body at that point in time; it is your body's coping mechanism.

So, if you want your brain to think happier, healthier,

more loving thoughts, then help it out a little by feeding your body happy healthy foods 80% of the time and indulging in the not so good foods 20% of the time. At least this is a balance tipped in everyone's favour. You get to indulge every now and then in Macca's, pies and pizza, yet the other 80% of the time your body is in cruise mode, enjoying functioning at its highest, happiest levels. So then, when you do indulge, it is strong enough to maintain that high energetic frequency which will keep you feeling good.

Unfortunately, in this day and age, we are a world who wants more, quicker, faster and now! This means man has had to intervene to keep up with our demands.

We are using pesticides and chemicals on the fruit and veg to make it grow faster and last longer on the shelves. We are injecting growth hormones into our chickens and meat to grow them faster, bigger and more meaty. We spray the grass and grain crops to grow them faster and keep the bugs off, and then the cows feed off the sprayed grain and grass which produces their milk faster.

So even so called "healthy" food, like fruit and veg, can be damaging when man has intervened in the process. This is why buying organic or local, farm fresh is super important; you don't want all of those

FOOD

nasty chemicals, pesticides, hormones and toxins in your body, wreaking havoc. Same goes with any man-made foods. Most likely these are constructed with such an array of fake numbers, chemicals, fillers and toxins that they are going to do more harm than good. Packets of flavouring you place on your noodles, over-processed, sugar laden sauces or anything that can survive in your pantry for years without going off is not healthy for your delicate and intricate insides. I get it, you're teens, eating junk is a part of your lifestyle, but what you need to understand is if you are constantly feeling shit, sad and sorry then understanding the "why am I feeling this way all the time?" will require you to look at what's not working or what is not balanced in your life right now. And because food is something we consume every single day, our feelings and moods can almost always be pinpointed back to our diets.

What did you eat yesterday? How much of it was manipulated by man? How much of it was good, happy, wholesome, energetic food straight out of the earth?

We are so lucky that WE get to choose how WE want to eat, and we also get to choose how WE want to feel. Feel good —> eat good, it's that simple.

WTF - I CANT EVEN DEAL

See, every time you eat or drink, you are either feeding your bad mood or fixing your bad mood, and that's a powerful thing to understand and have power over.

I could go on and on about food, diets and the rest of it, but if I was giving advice to myself growing up about the overwhelming food choices, diets and food fads out there, it would be this: DON'T OVER COMPLICATE FOOD. The simpler the food, the better for you.

- The more simple the label, the better for you.

- The more simple the source, the better for you. For example, a banana or a banana flavoured protein health bar? Choose the most simple form: the banana! Choose the item that has not been poked and prodded, added and packaged with fancy words like "high protein," "less fat," "get fit" or "lose this" garbage.

- Simple will always be best. If a label has words you can't even pronounce and numbers galore (306, 705…), then chances are it's not going to be as good as a salad sandwich or mum's homemade biscuits.

- Don't buy into the bull shit. People can't make millions off selling you an apple, but they can

FOOD

make millions off selling you an apple sauce laced with un-needed crap.

People can't make millions off selling you spinach, but they can make millions off selling you a spinach-based wonder powder that "makes you awesome."

- Eat simple, healthy, wholesome foods 80% of the time, and enjoy an indulgence when you feel called to do so.

- Drink lots of fresh water, not fake, sugar-laden soda.

- Think of your body as your car and fuel it with the right petrol, the good stuff, so it will drive you longer, keep you air conditioned and play you the right tunes for a happy and cruiser ride.

- If you feel shit, sad or sorry, emotionally and physically, it's time to look at your diet and make some changes—the simplest being simplify it!

- Start with cutting out sugar! Eating foods that are highly processed and filled with sugar is equivalent to popping a bad mood pill. When you consume excess sugar your body initially has superhero tendencies and can jump up and almost fly with all that energy. But what goes up must come down, and down you go, hitting harder and doing more damage, falling flat on your face. There is so much information out there: "don't eat this food or that food." And the biggest misconception is "don't eat fruit because it too contains too much sugar." The sugar in fruit is not the same sugar that is in your soft drink or cakes. The sugar in fruit is very much needed in your body to fuel your brain and muscles. It is used up within minutes of consuming it, zipping off around your body, making your muscles pump, your brain more alert, healing bad cells in your body and helping your mind stay happy and emotionally stable.

EAT GOOD, FEEL GOOD; EAT SHIT, FEEL SHIT
What mood are you serving yourself?

LET'S FIX THIS SHIT

LET'S FIX THIS SHIT

1. EXERCISE

You brush your teeth every day so they stay healthy and clean. You sleep every day so your body can rest. You eat every day so your body has fuel to keep you going. You shower every day so you feel clean. You are on your phone every day, who knows why. Then why don't you exercise or at least move your body every day?

We need to stop thinking of exercise as a chore or a bore. It is therapy for your body, mind and soul and an easy and free therapy at that. EVERYTHING functions better when you move your body.

Don't forget, your organs need flushing, draining and moving to help detoxify them, and they can't do that without you physically moving your lazy ass.

Your lymphatic system doesn't have an internal rubbish dump like most of your other bodily systems. It will keep getting more and more filled up and clogged with toxins collected from the air you breathe, the foods you eat and the waste inside your cells until you move your body. You literally need to jump up and down to help your lymphatic system physically drain itself, otherwise, you will get sick more often.

Remember, your brain is like the gutter of a roof and if you keep filling it up with an overload of crap it will eventually become blocked and overflow. Then, you will be stressed, overwhelmed, overworked, foggy, tired and burnt out because you haven't allowed for any drainage holes to release the water overflow—you haven't taken the time to unclutter your gutter.

What helps release that overflow and unclutter your gutter? Exercise does: sweating, allowing new energy and happy endorphins to flood your brain, allowing every system in your body to be flushed out from toxins.

When you breathe hard from exercise, or increase your respiratory rate, it expands your lungs and triggers your heart to pump more oxygenated blood through your entire body, all of your muscles and cells, which makes you new again, RENEWED.

Exercise is not just good for us from an aesthetic perspective, or how we look on the outside (healthy, toned, ripped etc.), it reflects that exact same thing on the inside, making our organs, brain, moods and cells also look and feel good, healthy, toned, ripped.

LET'S FIX THIS SHIT

Your heart is one big muscle and what happens when we don't train big muscles? They get flabby and less effective at their job. If you increase your heart rate via exertion you are ultimately giving your heart muscle a good workout, making it stronger and thus making you stronger in all aspects of your life, as your heart is the reason you exist.

Exercise is therapy for your body, inside and out, mind, body and soul. You can spend hundreds of dollars on medication a year, or you can exercise your body for free.

You don't have to be training hard seven days a week, but having an awareness of moving seven days a week is a must for a perfectly functioning vessel.

If you sit at your desk all day at school, then get up and move around every hour to get that blood flow circulating. Take the stairs instead of the lift. Get off your computer or phone and run around.

Do you know what one of the biggest health epidemics is today? It is not drugs or alcohol or bad food; it is SITTING. People are sitting around for too many hours a day, not moving their bodies, causing a huge array of health, heart and head issues: bad health, more cardiovascular disease and an increase in depression and mental health problems.

WTF – I CANT EVEN DEAL

It is proven that when you are in a shitty mood exercise will help get you out of your funk. It releases chemicals into your brain, like dopamine, a chemical that makes you happy. Where do you think the phrase "that's dope" comes from?

Exercise will also decrease your anxiety by overpowering those restless, edgy, jittery and uptight feelings with calming hormones like serotonin. Serotonin impacts every part of your body and is considered a natural mood stabiliser, making your mood swings less psycho. It also affects your appetite and digestion, sleep, memory, and sexual desire and function. That is one chemical you want to keep flowing, and exercise can do that for you.

You don't have to train like a star athlete every day to get the amazing feel-good benefits that exercise can give you. 20 minutes a day may help to reset your head, refuel your body and restart your engine. 20 minutes a day of sacrificing some mindless scroll-zombie, social media to make yourself feel better and un-clutter your gutter is well worth the opposed shitty feelings, don't you think? Go for a walk with the dog, a run, some yoga or stretching, and leave your phone at home. You don't need to prove to your followers that you did a training session. That actually takes away the pleasure and adds to the pressure. At least three days a week, just move for you, to medicate you inside and out because ONLY YOU CAN LOOK AFTER YOU.

No doctors, specialists, psychiatrists, family members, personal trainers, pills or Instagram influencers will take care of you. They can help, but only YOU CAN LOOK AFTER YOUR BODY, INSIDE AND OUT. YOU ARE YOUR BEST FIX!

2. BE A POSITIVE AND KIND PERSON

I can tell you right now, I didn't have a specific group of friends I sat with every day at school; I was a group hopper. I wanted to be friends with everyone and be a part of every group's fun. I didn't know it at the time but this served me very well. I was generally nice and kind to everyone and in return I gained respect and kindness from everyone. When drama was going down, it was time to hop over to the group having more fun. I am not saying you have to be like me, but being kind to everyone will definitely serve you in the long run. See, you're only in high school for six, or so, years, but those years can help determine and influence the rest of your life and opportunities. Imagine applying for a huge, life-changing job, opening the door and finding nerdy, fatty farts that you used to pick on at school sitting behind the desk as your potential new boss, because he or she became super successful outside of the confines of the school walls. Now

WTF - I CANT EVEN DEAL

who has the upper hand? Likely to say, you ain't getting the job, because you were a douche back in the day. But if you took the time and effort to be kind and friendly to everyone, equally, then you just got the job with a boss who never forgot how nice you were to them.

Every single person in this world is made differently, uniquely and equally. And to be a positive, kind person just means understanding this and accepting that difference is a good thing. The world would be a bore if everyone was the exact same, and that is why school life is so hard. You have to adhere to a certain persona to be cool at school, and those who start to show their differences and unique quirks are the ones belittled and picked on. Yet they are also the ones that will flourish outside of school because they were brave enough to embrace their individuality from the get go! Why do you think bullying occurs? Because the bully doesn't know who they are and wants to bring those who do down, so they can feel better about their unfound and lost selves.

You do not have to like everyone. In fact, sometimes your energy won't match some other people's energy, hence the term "we are polar opposites" which, in fact, is actual science. The people who grate on your nerves the most have different frequencies to you, and like a dog hearing a screeching siren, it hurts their ears. That is how you also feel towards some people and that is totally normal. All you have to do is be polite and move on. There is no need to be an ass or a bitch. It does not make you cooler or a better person to belittle another human being in any way or form. It belittles your soul and you are the one who has to sit in silence in your own thoughts at the end of the day.

So how can I be a positive, kind person?

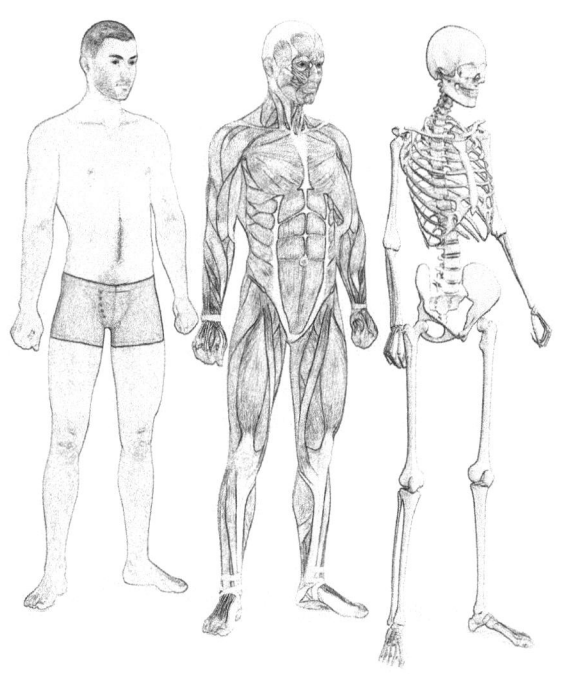

WTF - I CANT EVEN DEAL

Treat everyone as equal. If you could physically take off all of someone's skin we would all look exactly the same, like one of those muscle and skeleton dummies you see in science. Some would be big and tall and others short and small. Take off the outer shell and we are all extremely similar: heart, lungs, bones, muscles, liver, kidneys etc. The only thing that makes us different is our brain, as it creates our personalities and that's where issues of differences can arise.

What is a personality? Your personality is the combination of what you think and the emotions you feel as a result of those thoughts. You act out a certain behaviour that relates to those thoughts and emotions. You would be a very different person than you are today if from the day you were born you were locked in a white room with nothing else in it. You probably would just be a sitting heartbeat without many thoughts at all. Your personality forms during your childhood and is shaped through experiences and interactions within your environment: surroundings you grew up in, relationships you were influenced by, foods you ate, events that occurred around you, things you saw and things that were said to you. What you all need to understand is that none of you had control over those initial years. You probably only remember back to around six years of age and by that age your personality has been well influenced. What you do have control over is NOW! You control what you CHOOSE to be, do or say now, what and who you surround yourself with, how you eat, think and TREAT OTHERS now. As I said earlier, your schooling life will be a huge influence on the rest of your life, so choose wisely how you want that experience to be. It all works together to shape the person you are and will become in the big WIDE world—a very different place than school.

What you think and say most of the time is the direct reflection of your deep inner self. So, having an understanding about personalities can help you understand why people act the way they do, whether that be bullying and over powering, shy and timid, unique and weird, smart and quiet, loud and silly or bitchy and mean. That is why if someone was ever mean to me I never retaliated. I just thought to myself, "I feel sorry for that person, something has made them be like that and I know they are just trying to make themselves feel like a bigger and better person." So, I would just walk away, because the more power you give to negativity, the more you are feeding the weeds, like fertiliser, growing them and allowing them to take over your life. If you have negative thoughts towards someone, keep them to yourself. You don't have to like the person to be kind to them. Remember the boomerang: what you put out comes back at you. So be kind to others, and others will be kind to you!

Ok, ask yourself right now, what are my personality traits? Am I a positive, kind person and when was the last time I did something kind to another?

What sort of person do I want to be and want people to think of me, 20 years down the track?

What thoughts am I constantly thinking? Because that is what I am inviting into my life.

3. YOU ARE WHAT YOU THINK

We have touched on this topic in previous chapters, and the most important thing here to improve your overall happiness is to think happier and more positively. Yeah that sounds easier said than done, when it feels like the world is crumbling around you and all your brain wants to think is dark thoughts. But that is why I wrote this book: to help you stop feeling shit, sad and sorry.

Look around your space, your life and your world right now. What are you consuming your time with? You are what you see, what you do, what you eat, what you look at and what you surround your life and body with. Is it dark and negative or bright and fun?

LET'S FIX THIS SHIT

Social media. Are you following only positive people who make you feel good, and not people who bring you down and make you question your life and self? How many mind-numbing hours are you spending on social media, DISCONNECTED, not only to the world but to you, the you inside of you?

Are you engaging in too much negative influence? Are you paying too much attention to world events like war, hurt, sadness, death and violence? Are you engaging in too many parties, drugs and alcohol? Or are you having fun, reading, watching fun movies, being creative, going out into nature and enjoying life?

Do you allow yourself to be belittled and spoken down to? Do you hang around bitchy, nasty instigators or nice, friendly, fun people? Do you know your self-worth?

Are you eating processed, negative, unhealthy foods that your body can't use to fuel your brain? Or are you eating good, healthy, wholesome foods that will fill up your brain with happiness, energy and clear thinking?

Are you listening to what your body needs through this delicate, teenage, hormonal time?

Are you giving yourself time alone, creative time, fun time, sloth time, peaceful, quiet time, loud, crazy, energetic time? Your body will tell you if it is energetic and wants to run around or if it's sad and wants to be alone. LISTEN, don't fight it. Your body is always working with you and working to look after you without you even knowing the hard work it does internally for you.

4. ACUPUNCTURE

Acupuncture can help with any health issue, but is found to be really helpful with emotional and mental health because it affects brain chemistry. Acupuncture causes an increase in the production of those feel-good chemicals, like endorphins in the brain, which have a calming effect. It also resets the energy mojo in your body, like tuning into the right frequency for a particular radio station, and it has been known to help with many emotional conditions, including stress, anxiety, depression and panic attacks. If you have never had acupuncture before, it does not hurt in the slightest. In fact, you cannot even feel the tiny needles they use to generate and correct your energy flow and mojo. If you go ahead right now and give your arm a gentle pinch with your finger nails, the acupuncture needles would hurt less than that did.

5. MAINTAINANCE

Importantly if you feel shit, sad and sorry, check the list, ask why. What is stressing you out and weighing you down, making you unbalanced from head to toe? That is all that feeling low and crap most likely is: an overflowing gutter issue you haven't attended to for a while, which is now tapping you on the shoulder saying, "HEY, let's fix this by getting back into a steady flow again and balance things mentally, emotionally and physically."

I want you to understand, all of these issues we have spoken about are connected, interwoven and require attention and attending to. Just like a garden can look amazing when attended too and manicured, it can also become overgrown with weeds in a short period of time if unattended to, especially if there has been a downpour of rain, or in your case, a downpour of stress. You, your body and mind are no different. They can be taken over if not looked after.

You live with this one space called your body for the rest of your life. Don't you want to keep it in tip top working order so it can do the same for you? You cannot just choose one area to improve and think that will make you happier. You cannot just choose to eat healthy and hope you will feel better when you are stressed, overworked, not exercising, hormonal and on your phone 24/7. You have to take snippets of each category to bring together an overall balance of your moods and keep them stable. This is not a part-time job you do for a couple of months a year. It requires a lifetime of maintaining, correcting, adjusting, learning and cultivating to perfect your space.

IF YOU CHANGE NOTHING,
nothing changes!

IF YOU CHANGE NOTHING, nothing changes!

Not everyone is made the same. In fact, no two people are made the same. Everybody is different. Emotions, needs, wants, health, happiness and illnesses are very individualised.

This book is a simple guide to help unravel how certain factors in our lives can contribute to our emotional state of wellbeing, our overall health and happiness. Some of you may have amazing success tracking these factors and gaining back control over these issues, and others may try them all and still feel exactly the same. The important thing to learn and take away from this book is only you know how you feel, and only you can really help yourself by taking some control over your body, mind and soul. Gather information, seek help and try different avenues, but understand that IF YOU CHANGE NOTHING, nothing changes!

It all starts with you speaking up and telling someone you don't feel right, whether that is physically or emotionally. Then, you forge a plan to get help, and, importantly, you help yourself feel well. By reading this book I hope you won't be so hesitant in speaking up about feeling shit, sad and sorry. IT'S NORMAL. We all feel this way, and now, hopefully, you understand the "why" behind feeling this way and that it is a good thing. It is our body saying, "hey, I want to help you but I need you to change something, do more or less of something." It is your little engine light coming on, wanting to make you better... LISTEN. All the emotions and "WTF I can't even deal" with life can be as simple as your hormones being out of whack or your vitamins and minerals needing a boost. Just because we feel crap does not mean we are mentally sick and need locking away or medication to make us better. The issues I have covered are normal, everyday struggles every single human on the planet has to deal with, manage and figure out. We all have it in us to feel well, and I hope this book can be your starting point, your emotional manual to feeling the way you are meant to feel when your body is working in a perfect balance with your mind, body and soul.

THE CHECK LIST

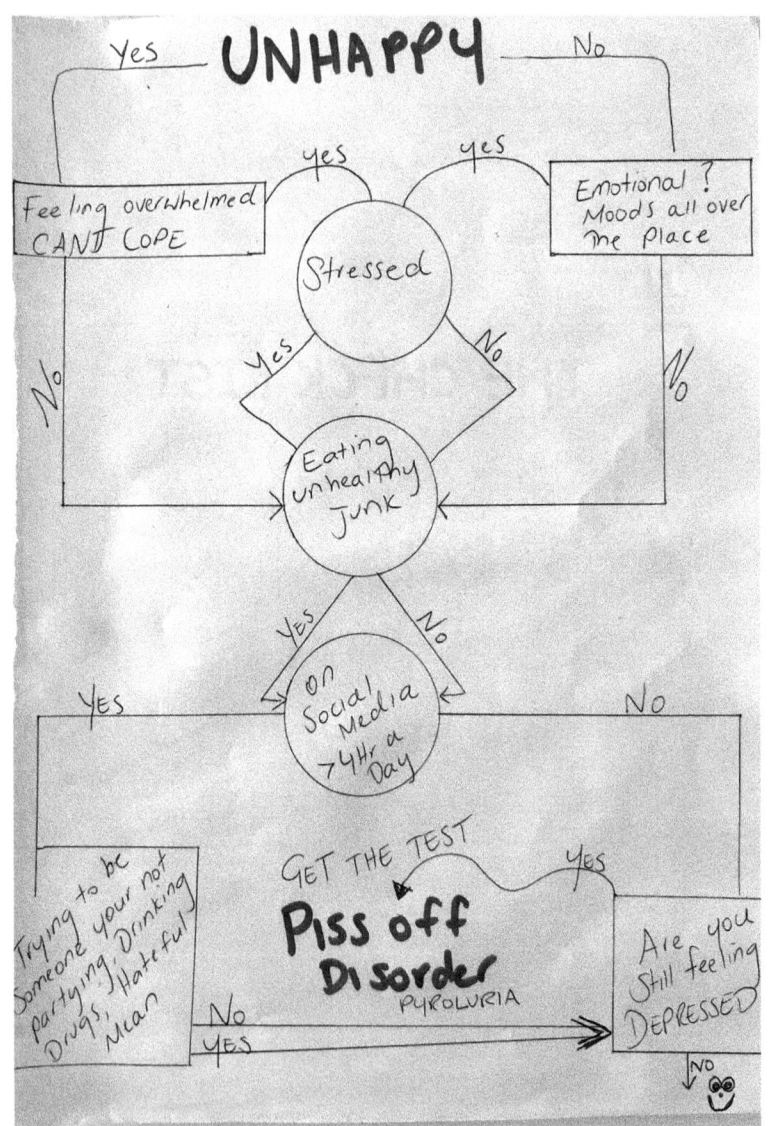

Food & Diet
- → Healthy ✓ ☺
- → Unhealthy — not enough Vitamins, nutrients & minerals like B6 can cause shitty moods! ☹

Exercise
- → Yes regularly ✓ ☺
- → No Exercise — Not releasing good endorphins & toxic build up within the Body & Brain

Social Media online →
- < Less Than 3Hr a Day ☺
- > More Than 3Hr a Day ☹
  - Zoning out, disengaging disconnecting from the real world. Comparing, dulling down the Brain's intellect!

Stress & Pressure
- → Not Stressed ☺
- → Very Stressed = increase in HPL stress Hormone. Depleting vital nutrients That help keep us happy Sickness and inability to Think straight ☹

Hormones
- ～～▶ Normal & Balanced ☺
- ～～▶ Unbalanced — can cause emotional disturbances due to lack of secreting hormones ☹

This list is something you can always come back to whenever you are feeling off balance. Go through the list and see what needs fixing. It is my wish to see you happy, smiling and being silly!

Life is short

You only get to live it once

There are no do overs. You can only be in this moment once.

Choose fun
Choose free
Choose you

You are so extraordinary because

There is only one you

AND THAT IS FOR A REASON

You are meant to be here! You were made for this earth at this time for a special reason.

It's not a coincidence. You are a part of the magic.
It's destiny and your living your destiny right this minute.

so

Do what makes you smile, what lights up your soul
because that will lead you to your REASON

ENJOY IT
EVERY LAST SECOND OF IT.

Let's stay in touch and support one another by using the
hashtag #wtficantevendeal on Instagram.

Upload your own smiley face pic like this one to support one another's journey through depression, mental illness and teen life in general. When we know we are not alone and can reach out to others going through similar problems it can make life a little easier.

And thank you, by purchasing this book you have helped bring more awareness to mental health, bullying and the everyday issues teenagers face online and in ones own head space.

A percentage of your purchase will be circulated to helping kids further realise their awesomeness through amazing programs like:

- Horses helping humans. A horse Whispering Youth Program. Helping youth develop their own character and personality developed by Sue Spence.
- Exercise and mental illness programs
- And selected youth charities like R U OK

You can follow me via @sweatseeker on Instagram or
www.sweatseeker.com.au

I'd love to see you all enjoying and sharing the book.

X x Ellice

www.ingramcontent.com/pod-product-compliance
Lightning Source LLC
Chambersburg PA
CBHW051945160426
43198CB00013B/2311